WHERE THE BLACK SWANS SWIM

Emily Barker is an award-winning Australian singer-songwriter. She had early success as the writer and performer of the theme to BBC/PBS Masterpiece crime drama Wallander starring Kenneth Branagh and has since gone on to forge an acclaimed catalogue of releases. Barker has released music and toured as a solo artist as well as with various bands and collaborations. She has written for TV and film, including composing the soundtrack for Jake Gavin's lauded debut feature Hector starring Peter Mullan. *Where the Black Swans Swim* is her debut collection of poems.

CONTENTS

NOTE: Australian Aboriginal and Torres Strait Islander peoples are advised that this document contains names of people who are deceased.

ISBN: 978-1-916938-28-1

Cover designed by Aaron Kent

Edited and Typeset by Aaron Kent

Broken Sleep Books Ltd
PO BOX 102
Llandysul
SA44 9BG

Where the Black Swans Swim

Emily Barker

Broken Sleep Books

ROBB JETTY

C.Y. O'Connor Beach, Western Australia

Hoof, heart & snout
once lipped this shoreline common as weed.

Sea then was blood & offal
        sharks paunchy.

On the beach, people walk dogs.
Imagine them unleashed in the past:

Pug gummed with oxen clots
        once-white Poodle dyed deep red
Staffy with a second tongue

        Kelpie herding drowned sheep
in cahoots with Golden Retriever
who hauls sodden fleeces to shore.

        Springer Spaniel flushes out
shaking lamb from behind an acacia
        English Pointer draws
all daggered eyes towards them

& sated mouths of mongrels
grin through red-tipped teeth
at bleating owners tethered

to weightless leashes, dry biscuits
unable to compete with cheek, fat, marrow.

Imagine one morning only morsels
lolling in the waves –

old abattoir chimney shivers.
Wolf remembered as jaw closes on bone.

PLACEHOLDER

Plankton farts detected on an alien planet
was the subject line of an email today.
Planet was K2-something. Its surface
covered in water, perhaps.

I turned on a tap to make this rooibos
& water poured out, into the kettle
which shook as I sent messages
prepped the pot.

If we make water go somewhere it wasn't, do we create thirst in the desert?
There are wars in my phone where I order more of what water helped make.

I'll imbibe & go to the beach, watch the dog
watch the statue of C.Y. O'Connor on a horse
barnacles a-bling with the sucked-out tide
cormorant on his head.

Mum calls about a collective present for my 2 y/o niece
but I'm in debt fucking up my home, assuming you all
want to fix things too – & for the life of me I can't
figure out what to buy to stop these endings.

Atoms – yours are mine, Remember?[1]
To wipe cement dust from tiny cheeks, find mothers –

Will we war in slow motion on our new earth?
I'm thinking of astronauts.
The futures we let –
The futures –

There's a graveyard for wind turbines
a Chuck Berry record on the moon & Ayva
up to her chin in Indian ocean, whimpering
at shit-covered bronze.

Not even the past isn't moving –
Read this –   *See?*

After a swim
absurdity in the shower
            washing salt
from my living arms.

SEA FREQUENCIES

sherbet on cells *pianissimo* through skull
aspirin diss- in champagne glass

two thousand hertz of salt kiss smack
sand as ocean ⟹

in belly of wave shellcrush & stone
sailor bones, barnacled trees

tenor-voiced call of calcified mids
somewhere between shore & C3

bass string *ff*lap, guttural thud
of kick drum on taut real estate

thunder of tympanic membrane
subwoofs on westerly wind

& beyond our audition ⁊   ultrasong
scored through teeth of sperm whales

lim sup, lim inf, lim sup, lim inf, lim sup
dimin-   ø

ROTTNEST ISLAND DAISIES

Below ground

        364 skeletons
     in foetal position
knee caps to mandibles
  femurs to ribs
     knuckles   loose
       teeth   adrift
         in salt-dry soil

                    74,984 bones

                    I don't miss a wink
                         pitch tent, zip, unzip

        no circles etched in bark
        no mounds burnt by funeral fire
        no grave –

            tourist plaques
            offset slavery
            at *place across the water*
            where prisoners quarried limestone
            built their own cells   (now hotel rooms)
                the roads   this sea wall
                lighthouse

                where I holiday
                like there was no yesterday

CAN I SAY HER PHOTOGRAPH?

Her sand has sun set in its grit
        is homelands in bucket, her palm –

gift from bomb-littered birth shore
where mob was moved on for war.

Sheds crocodile song for distant Country
each note a grain for ancestors, childhood

of salt & moonslip down Mindil beach.
Corporal Dolly Gurinyi Batcho –

        an ocean pooled
two bobby pins in her black hair

Larrakia leader, un-enlisted backbone
        fifty years from home

more than one war to win.

KNOWLEDGE

If a swarm of strangers
tore down all my street signs
would I know the way
home by heart?

If my word for home
was forbidden
would my story stay
safe in the new noun?

If I had six seasons
& two of them were silenced
would flowers go on blooming
in a nameless time of year?

If my word for pregnant woman
was *boodjari*
& my word for earth
found within her womb

would I tread more lightly
across the stolen *boodjar*
dry the river
pump poison in her veins?

With what words do I build
bridges over rapids?
If *kaartdijin* is one of them
I begin building here.

RIVER SONG

Her first name was buried
    beneath branches, granite, bones

      in a bed of black silt
        words gurgle –

       Goor

            bil

            i

            yup

       Goorbiliyup – large intestine –
         bestowed in language
         River remembers

      Her drowned nouns are six seasons
           that mouthed moods of rain
         blushed birthing flowers
        clocked moulting swans

     Gone – words for eyes
    through which to see
      the nuance of a year
   dressing, disrobing
     the stolen land around us

Her rapids roar in *Noongar*:
Boodjari – pregnant woman –
& wombed within this word
word for earth – *Boodjar*
soil, a soul
fragile as a foetus

Bib

bul

mun

Bibbulmun –

place of plenty
Southwest – shape of breast *(bib)*
where for centuries, River sated
every mouth from here to sea

& what words mean, will be

Bridgetown –
tainted water
under a wooden bridge
where abundance used to breathe

THYLACINE THEORIES

After monsoons were silenced
& parched lakes shrunk to salt beds

After packs of dingoes swept red sands
for the same pouched & feathered prey

After we took smoking sticks
to grassed & wattled understorey

folded sails of thieving boats away
then booted, stepped onto drying land

After we blew bullets into pelted meat
& men, penned in our livestock

After chunks of chickens & lambs
were strewn across treeless paddocks

After the extinction of Tasmanian hens
we put a bounty on their fox-like heads

After their popularity on zoo stage
 where none of them bred

After the last one in captivity, Benjamin
got locked out of his shelter in a storm

& without the mammalian warmth of another
 died

we see him, black & white –
    theory pacing a cage.

GLOSSARY OF AN AUSTRALIAN MAGPIE

Gymnorhina –
genus (its very own) &
of the *Artamidae* family –
songs birds that are
> four octaves &

tibicen –
piper / flautist
fifer / player
can vary pitch over

mimic
native & introduced birds
humans & sirens
dogs, horses

> (creation song carolled
> through dying embers
> of night fire
> as slow light glides
> over & down the hill)

Omnivorous –
insects, earthworms, snails
rubs stingers off bees & wasps
rubs hairs off caterpillars before swallowing
eats poisonous cane toads by flipping
them on their backs & tearing
out their underparts
finds larvae of scarab beetles
by vibration
& for this reason is thanked by farmers

Synanthrope –
abides car fumes & fire
concrete & rose gardens
will remember you
for offerings of steak & other kindnesses
then won't swoop
even when nestlings
writhe pink & blind in a bed

of coat hangers & headphones
at the top of a telephone pole

some die by electrocution
some by windshield
rodenticides
& bastards who shoot them

if a parent dies
koolbardi adopts cooperative parenting
helper birds hop in
assist with feeding, raising the young

"It's not just a Noongar story, it's a West Australian story because we all call this place home" – Gina Williams[2]

Noongar –
Indigenous people of the south-west of Australia who first named

Koolbardi –
symbol of healing, story of sky
too close to the ground
when trees could not grow
& people had to crawl
birds had to walk
until *koolbardi* took long sticks
in blue/grey beak
pushed up & up until the sky
threw itself open & sun spilled
over the land to birth the first sunrise

SOUTHWEST SONNET

~~baarang~~ branch   ~~ngoolyark red-tailed black cockatoo~~   ~~dalyal green leaves~~

          ~~baarang branch~~   ~~manitjinmat white cockatoo~~

~~baarang branch~~   ~~mopoke owl~~   ~~meetcha honkey nuts~~   koolbardi magpie

          baarang branch   boort bark   goomalling place of possums

baarang branch   mayat red sap   dalyal green leaves

          baarang branch   djilyaro bees   koolbardi magpie

      ~~baarang branch~~   ~~boorn tree~~   ~~doongkoorlanwort fall over~~

      ~~boort bark~~   ~~mia-mia shelter~~   karl fire   karl fire

  kara spider   djert little bird   karl fire

      wetij emu   ~~karl fire~~   fire   fire   fire

  karda bandicoot   fire   fire   fire   fire   fire

~~boorn~~ log   ~~yoorn~~ bobtail lizard   fire   fire   fire

boodjera ground   boya rock   bilara dry leaves   fire   ~~boololoant~~   fire fire fire   ~~nadjiny yolk of an~~

~~egg~~

21

ERASURE SONNET

'Australia: Capital of mammal extinction…' - Margaret Davis, The Science Times, 4 March 2021

broad-faced potoroo   toolache wallaby

thylacine   the marl   desert bettong   blue

-grey mouse   capricorn rabbit-rat   percy

island flying fox   southern bent wing bat

leadbeater's possum   dibbler   bilby

queensland northern hairy-nosed wombat

gilbert's potoroo   monjon   woylie

christmas island pipistrelle   kangaroo

island dunnart   northern quoll   koala

gould's mouse   numbat   long-footed potoroo

quokka   feral cat   kangaroo island echidna

rabbit   boar   camel   horse   goat   european

red fox   human

SOUND OF EMPTINESS

Kilometres of stretched coral   off-white
                as old ship's sails
                        where no shrimp crackle
        like bacon in well-oiled pans
                no fizz belch chatter pop   whizz   whoosh
of squid   of ray   of baby blue whales
        breaching oceans away   of jellied otherleys
                        of seahorse
        or tortoise
                no schools of shy angel fish dash for shelter
                        in rainbowed fingers
                                waving
                                like crowds of fans towards their star

                Boneyard.   Muted but for the brief thud
                                of diver's heart in funeral of sea

#BUSHFIRES

Blue wren fossicks
through white ash
in burnt-out forest.

On our way to the beach
you pull over for
a closer look –

iPhone angled just above eye-level
you snap a curation
by still-smoking trees.

Back in the car, barely a word
for dead animals
razed understorey.

Blue wren flies off
we leave the monochrome

you thinking of captions
me thinking of babies

switched at birth –

> *I knew this trip*
> *wasn't about swimming.*

HORSE NATIONS

The only light in this valley
comes from our bathroom
where we've shared water
now stand on the oak chest
four of us in towels in a line
with Dad, a horse yelling
bedtime! I dig spurs into ribs
canter the corridor
jump fallen eucalypts
      jump fallen bodies
      I don't yet know are there
swim rapids, hoof it down cliffs
on a dun national symbol like
'Man from Snowy River'
      (poem & film with one white fallen body
      (& if Paterson's lead was Indigenous
      'The Brumby Wars' is on its haunches
      with pros: SEE, MYTH FOR EVERYONE!
      & nos: BUT THE SCREAMING LAND!))
then exhausted at the station
Dad bucks me into bed, gallops off
rebirths into a black swan
that glides my sister to sleep
in a room with eroded walls.

SWAN BREWERY

Rainbow serpent, *Waugul,* made hills
& silted bed for *Derbal Yerrigan* –
where black swans swim & salt red bills
& ocean beckons river towards sand.
Place where *Whadjuk* families camped
to drink clean water from hillside spring.
To trade in ochre, eat *gilgies,* stamp
cindered ground for *moolyeet,* songs that link

lodestars to land. *Goonininup,* home
for sixty thousand years then *BAM!*
Flour mill. Tannery. Brewery. Ruins. Loan
to Labour party. Political scam.
Protest. Police. People behind bars.
Table with a view. Pink champagne. Cigar.

OODGEROO

Oodgeroo Noonuccal, also known as Kath Walker, was the first Indigenous Australian woman to publish a book of poetry.

Oodgeroo (paperbark tree, rooted in her name)
blows words from under the shade of a white alias.

Cyclone breath of black butterflies whisk
neon blue & rust as skin of Australia peels back.

A continent's worth of dust rises, empire's worth
of buried voices become storm.

Sentences scratch at borders of exile. Paperbark
sheds pages, letters arranged on painted placards

in poems, speeches – anywhere words will grow.
Shoved under closed doors, shouted down streets.

A demand: read me as a citizen of my country!
            Cocooned in her name, Oodgeroo's ink

                  finds home before blood or bone
                  in print across the red-dirt nation.

Where now are words that spell freedom?
Not in school books or shelves in homes.

You have to dig deeper than you should –
where the water table rises & dirt turns wet

her words lap at roots of ghostly paperbark
            read me, read me, read me.

STILL LIFE WITH WRITING DESK

She looks up from words, sees river.
Postcard mirror. Eye level. Misted.
Autumn she thinks. Wipes sleeve
across surface, herself still there.

Beneath postcard, petals fall.
Ascension into memory
through dried roses crushed
like lovers under soft light
of an aureate lamp. Desktop garden

where flood themes flood themselves
(her river, endless question of home)
in black rivulets across sodden page.
She sits, cornered by Cotswold stone
old as white ghosts at Botany Bay.

Outside it's dark already. New winter
scrapes fingernail branches down glass.
She writes reasons why she stays away.
With missing, a constant source of rain.

Stroud, UK

WHERE THE BLACK SWANS SWIM

for Jon the Boatman

There's a hatch in my backyard
beneath the shade of the shedding paperbark
that I open on days when I want to drink pints
at the bar with you & argue about Neil Young.

I close the door behind me
descend foot-worn stone
enter by the piano where the jazz band play
their thirty yearlong version of Bad Penny Blues.

It's been so hot up there
I almost stopped believing in snow.
I can see it now, falling on narrowboats
& twined white swans that sleep
by Regents Canal.

You get the first round.
I talk about bushfires
Indian Ocean swims
how good the coffee is
no matter which cafe you go in.

A gardener, you ask what grows
in the sandy soils above, *Melaleuca*
I say & point to roots
that dangle like a grove
of tangled chandeliers.

You talk about Charlie Oak – your baby boy –
named for Charlie Rich & your favourite tree
about new old gems you've found on Spotify:
Jimmy Liggins & His Drops of Joy, The Swan
Silvertones, Kate Wolf, Fats & Buddy.

On pint three we file a complaint
about the lights: too bright.
We've seen this pub at half candescence
be a lantern for souls coming in from the cold:

overworked architects, families from the estate
CAMRA tickers, narrowboaters
& ghosts who couldn't quite
say goodbye.

The bell for last orders chimes.
We nod to Jackie who refills our glasses
& as is custom, end on Elvis:
his Comeback Special affirms we must
stride towards *a sky more blue.*

The band latch instruments into sticky cases.
I wobble upstairs to the carol of waking magpies
open the hatch to a world of sunlight
where no hangovers or heart attacks spill into the day.

Where soon I'll walk my nephew
to the school by the warm lake
that brims with black swans
luminous as present tense.

GLOSSARY

Noongar (also spelt **Noongah, Nyungar, Nyoongar, Nyoongah, Nyungah, Nyugah**) are the First Nations people of the south west of Australia. In Noongar language, the Southwest is **Bibbulmun** Country meaning 'place of plenty'. Some of the poems in this pamphlet integrate Noongar words, which are translated below.

Boodjar: earth
Derbal Yerrigan: Swan River, Perth
Gilgies: freshwater crayfish
Kaartdijin: knowledge
Koolbardi: Australian magpie
Moolyeet: initiation rites
Wadjemup: Rottnest Island's original name meaning 'place across the water'
Waugul: the great rainbow snake of Noongar Dreaming
Whadjuk: name of the dialectal Noongar group from the Perth area

ENDNOTES

1.   after Maya Angelou
2.   Gina Williams quote – 'WA Opera premieres Noongar saga Koolbardi wer Wardong' – The West Australian, 7th Oct 2021

ACKNOWLEDGEMENTS

With thanks to Adam Horovitz, Vanessa Lampert, Dr Fran Lock, Anthony Anaxagorou, The Poetry School, CurtinX: Noongar Language and Culture course, Lukas Drinkwater & Howard Mills.

Thanks to these places for publishing these poems first:
Robb Jetty – *Magma Poetry Magazine* #86 'Food'

Sea frequencies – longlisted for the *Mslexia* Poetry Competition 2023

Can I say her photograph? (previously 'Native Title') – shortlisted for The Plaza Poetry Prize

Knowledge – shortlisted for the *Aesthetica* Creative Writing Award: Poetry 2022

River song – longlisted for the *Australian Book Review*'s Peter Porter Poetry Prize 2022

Oodgeroo – *Quadrant* May 2017

Still life with writing desk – *192 Magazine*

Where the Black Swans Swim – Poetic Map of Music, Southwark Libraries

LAY OUT YOUR UNREST